R.A.W.

08 JUN 2023

PATIENCE AGBABI

Gecko PRESS

Patience Agbabi was born in London in 1965. She was educated at Pembroke College, Oxford and the Performance Poetry Scene, London. She lives in London and works as a writer, performance poet and workshop coordinator in the UK and abroad. This is her first poetry collection.

R.A.W.

Copyright © Patience Agbabi 1995

ISBN: 0 9524067 1 3

First published 1995 by
Izon Amazon
in association with
Gecko Press
30B Stanmer St
Battersea
London SW11 3EG

Cover photograph by A. D. Curwen
Hair design by Frankie at Aquarius
Graphic design by Dave Baxter at Neal's Yard DTP

Printed in Great Britain by
Antony Rowe Ltd, Wiltshire.

Special thanks to my family and friends;
Ahmed Sheikh, Regina Bufkin, Merle Collins,
Brother Niyi, Pitika Ntuli, Hackney Black Writers,
Hackney Women Writers, The Federation of Worker
Writers & Community Publishers, Vertical Images,
Apples & Snakes, The Hard Edge Club, Survivors
Poetry, World Oyster Club, Blue Nose Café, Hackney
Empire, Adeola Agbebiyi, Anita Naoko Pilgrim,
Benjamin Zephaniah, Lemn Sissay, Free Speech,
Martin Glynn, Attila the Stockbroker, The Voice Box,
Chris 'Rap' Brown, Dave Harrington, Word Express;
and Jade, John, Adrian and Dave at Gecko Press.

Many thanks to the students and teachers at the
schools, colleges and universities for their hard work
and creativity.

R.E.S.P.E.C.T. to freestyle e.V.; Linda Bernhardt,
Cheryl Sack, Lesego Rampolokeng and Music Ye
Africa; Sapphire; Mala Seecoomar, The Nuyerican
Poets, Rachel Paul and the women of Scandinavia;
and Lennie St Luce and Bunie Sexwale.

This book is dedicated to freedom of speech

Acknowledgements

These poems have been previously recorded and published in the following:

'One Hell of a Storm' was recorded on compilation CD/LP *One Hell Of A Storm* (Tongue & Groove) 1994 and performed on LBC Radio in 1990. It was published with 'Serious Pepper' and 'My Mother' in *Frankenstein's Daughter* (Stride) 1993. 'Serious Pepper' first appeared in its original form in *The Popular Front Of Contemporary Poetry* (Apples & Snakes) 1992; and 'My Mother' in *Writing Women* 8:2/3 1991 and as a poster (Centerprise Publications) 1992. 'Sex Is' was performed on Radio 5 in 1991 and published in *Words from the Women's Cafe* (Centerprise Publications) 1993. It was published with original versions of 'Money Talks', 'Sentences' and 'It's Better Post- than Pre-' in *Wake Up* 11, 1994. 'Rappin It Up' was performed on DEF II, BBC2 in 1992 and published in *The Virago Book Of Wicked Verse* (Virago Press Ltd) 1992. 'RAPunzel' was published in *Doin Mi Ed In* (Pan Macmillan Children's Books) 1993. 'R.A.W.' was performed on TV1, Radio Metro and Radio 702 in South Africa, 1994.

CONTENTS

Introduction by Merle Collins 9

Accidentally Falling 11
My Mother 12
Serious Pepper 14
From Green to Red to Black 17
We Press Buttons 18

One Hell of a Storm 20
0 22
Ode Intimations of DM ortality 24
The Black The White and The Blue 26
Sentences 28
Cain 31
E (Manic Dance Mix A) 33

Miss First World 34
Becoming A Nonymous 36
London's Burning 38
It's My Party 41
Blonde Bombshell Defused 44
Money Talks 46

R.A.W. 48
Rap Trap 51
Stings Like a Bee 53
RAPunzel 54
Sex Is 56
It's Better Post- than Pre- 58
Rappin It Up 61

Introduction

The title of this collection R.A.W. is an expression of the intensity with which Patience Agbabi has occupied the stage, reading and performing her work in Britain and abroad during the 1990s.

Coming of age in London during the years of Thatcherite British politics, Patience has increasingly used the poetic medium to dialogue with reality as Black, as British, as woman, as individual deeply affected by the negativities of racism, sexism, homophobia and general intolerance. With this publication, Patience Agbabi has become one of the poets whose work invites analysis in both print and performance.

On stage her work has moved from a quiet, almost tentative expression at the end of the 80s to a mesmerizing assertiveness in the 90s, as she constructs a response to the attitudes that inform the society which has shaped her. This is poetry in the tradition of social commentary, informed by techniques of the oral performance mode discussed in various ways by writers and critics such as Ngugi Wa Thiong'o, Ruth Finnegan and Walter Ong. One senses that Patience is continuously on her way to deeper examination of the issues that inform her existence.

On stage, as she works with various rhythms for effect and constructs a delivery to engage the audience, she is obviously conscious of a social dimension in her role as performance poet, of a dimension to be spelt out particularly in her role as woman performance poet. As she says in R.A.W. ;

> "I don't want to attract
> only to attack..."

and again,

> "...no time to pause
> I'm a poet
> it's a four letter word".

On the page, poems such as *Accidentally Falling, My Mother, One Hell Of A Storm, E* and *Miss First World* clearly depend on the written medium for dimensions of their effect, so that as poet, Patience Agbabi moves easily from one form to another, inviting appreciation of her work in both print and performance.

In its themes, this collection is a sensitive exploration of the various aspects of duality in the expression and experiencing of identity: being Nigerian and British, becoming and not becoming one's mother, being considered very English and very un-English in speech and attitude. Characters exist in and outside of society, in and out of the closet, as 'respectable' citizens with skeletons in their cupboards.

In various ways the collection raises questions about identity, about the face presented to the world, about the face constantly reshaped by the world and about the deeper realities of existence. It urges the reader to think of the complexities which are constantly shaping individual responses and affecting collective attitudes.

Here in print, the reader is presented with a vibrant voice which is becoming increasingly more powerful on the performance poetry scene in Britain and abroad.

Merle Collins
July 1995

Accidentally Falling

Cheers
to the not
so distant
past They
always say
the first
sip is the
accidentally
falling in
lust period
Had we never
met each other
happened to fall
together entwined
I would not vintage
that bitter-sweet taste of
lips met over a glass of wine
experience ninesummersrolled
deliciously into our one green
bottle Caressed by the waves
we went the way of all lovers
when tipsy swaying to the hum of
summer bees our lust dried up
ran through fingers like sand
We noticed one-another's faults
your eyes took on that half-empty
half-hearted all is over look
You laughed when my jokes were
serious I cried when we were
bodily united mentally untied
tossing on a grey pebble beach
desperate scraping the barrel
making it up only to quarrel
making nothing but memories
drew the whole thing out until
it was out of control finished
sentimental dust I relive it
annually smiling vacant over
a bottle of wine now it's over
past just like the other nine

My Mother

My mother   has two heads
speak   alien tongue
their words   flow in
one ear   in the other
battle   in heart
head   know better
bolder   wiser older

My mother   married at 16
24   long time ago
where water   was unsafe
to drink   frozen solid
had chilblains   children
sang under coconut chestnut
save yourself   they say
for a rainy day   be bold
chic   rouge on the cheek
out out   you must go
say   no

Study hard   you read
too much   I never see you
always out   reading wearing
drab clothes   I miss you
so much   be proud
of your colour   culture
don't be different difficult
find a nice   Black
African man   no hurry
tomorrow   will do
go out   or no-one
will notice you   that there is no-one
my mother   cannot believe

My mother thrusts
thrusts her womanhood
onto me and my nipples
cannot quite focus
cannot quite breathe
then I am stronger
fight against her battle
she loves hates
my strength we share
a common resentment
common battle
painfully I emerge
an adult The following

day   allies in conflict we stride bareheaded
I am no longer single   she
seeing in me herself   in her self me

Serious Pepper

Everyone's born
no-one's found
until they find themselves

hurting in the back of the throat
because they've swallowed
serious pepper   painful as truth

I used to eat cold meals all the time
they had been hot
once

but they held my nose and force
fed me on two cultures
egg and chips or eba and groundnut stew

nothing got past the
lump
in my throat

In Sussex they used to say
'You don't pronounce it like that
in England...did you pick that up from your

parents?'   And in London
'Your cockney voice is so ugly
why can't you speak properly?'

And so often 'You're so English
I want to squeeze the Englishness
out of you'   Yes

Too Black   Too White
in limbo   on the edge
of the dance floor   playing gooseberry

but not found under a gooseberry bush
I knew who my parents were
they natured and they nurtured me

You can never forget that they love you
in spite of it all   In the 70s
I stopped playing

with dolls and began with words
red words   green words   yellow words
if I rubbed my eyes they stung me

I was desperate
        disparate
        diasporate

Someone said recently
'It's always good to remember details
from the past'

but I'm always afraid
of serious pepper
painful as truth

D'you know I used to stick my fingers down
my throat so I didn't have to grow up
and find myself

in spite of that my bust remained
it stopped growing at the age of 12
but it grew heavier

The Pill fills an empty bra quite nicely
and gives you the freedom
to fuck up your body

Serious pepper is two bodies rubbing
together beneath the sheets
making more noise than love

Serious pepper is the grinding
of black on black or black on white
or white on black

The man   to a weighed down heart
is a way out
until the lump in the throat

means you can't talk about
what you want to   serious pepper
Suddenly you're toothless again

learning to speak your first words
Mummy   Daddy   joined in bed
how could you predict the future?

You eat pepper soup on Monday
baked potatoes on Tuesday
Wednesday morning they say

'Nigerian English!
Sounds like you have an identity problem
people will think you're mixed race'

I compromise with 'Nigerian British'
cos belongings are unimportant
but belonging is   Everyone's born

No-one's found until
they find themselves hurting
in the back of the throat

From Green to Red to Black

It is too late in time
    too late to pluck
      he loves me   he loves me not
      from their fragrant faces

    because we grow from green
      to red
          to black
but forget we not our roots
roots that mirror branches
our roots are our fruit

Green and small and sour
    I repel the love that means no harm
My small
    hard
    heart afraid to beat
      that word
      in case it breaks

    a clenched fist
    against the sun and rain that feed me
    yet feel the roots
    push up from green
    to red
      red
        dripping
      and my nipple bud
          face colour
          lips fill with love
          dripping
          and they reach to pluck
             and face colour hot
          from red to black
             BLACK
             and green and red
             complete

We Press Buttons

Yesterday on the beach
in an erogenous zone
we had a 90s experience
in black and white

Swam naked in
the champagne froth of the sea
and fell back onto
black crushed velvet sand
like the night that came upon us
like drunkenness

The moon
lit up the contours of the night
pulled back the tide
too hot for covers
we rolled on this relentless bed until
we slept like starfish
in perfect shadow

Today technicolour dawn
breaks the champagne bottle
leaving no romantic message

Thick frothy scum
throws up
bright supermarket packaging
multi-coloured used condoms
strange sea creatures

Someone on the promenade stares at
our black and white held hands and
in daylight colour becomes an issue

God in his designer
blue and white polka dot tie
admires the upward curves on
the company profit chart
lights a thick yellow cigar and
sinks deep into a plump office chair
pleased with his creation

The almost red desert sand
is consumed with tents and tanks
on all channels

We press buttons
hoping to escape
in black and white adverts

One Hell of a Storm

There's gonna be one hell of a storm
cos the sky is the colour of dust
and the bee hum stop mid
flight between Summer
and Autumn   drums
thunder my temple
I am a woman
about to
erupt
like
a

volcano
There's gonna be
one hell of a storm
cos the sun stop but the heat hangs
heavy like tarpaulin
The elements clash
a huge raised spiked fist
splits open ever
lasting sky
Black

clouds heavy
with burden
of urban dust and waste
and pain too long   hail
that same hell
There is blood
blood on my hands
as I wash   rinse
blood with
blood

The sky
that everlasting
vast expanse of nothing
that everyone and no-one
really believed in
blue or white or red
is gone to dust

No rainbows here
the elements have clashed
no water   no air   no ozone layer
the elements have clashed
like cymbals symbolic of Super Powers
the elements have clashed

The heat hangs heavy
in our heads
we know how to stop
we know how to stop
we know how to stop
the finger of regression
pressing us back

down
into the
earth our own
so that finger
can own the earth
For we are seeds
and nature is on our side
We bleed daily somewhere
somewhere raise our fists alone but

stop
can you hear the drums
thunder in your head?
There's gonna be
one hell
of a storm

0

Fetish
fascist
fashion
velvet
sandpaper
papier-mâché
0
is naked
from the nape up
nubile
nubian
nude
old man
on his deathbed
in a toupee
neo-nazi
national front
in combat
anti-nazi
in back to front
baseball cap
heads
stripped to bone
in a concentration camp
queers
in a cool
nightclub
niggas
with a natural
chic
alison limerick
seal
sinead

shinehead
skinhead
shaved head
non hirsute
erotic
exotic
0
is that bumble-bee
bush baby ecstasy
0
is the number
of the
narcissistic
90s
nearing
millennium
after 999
000

Ode   Intimations of DM ortality

There was a time when every DM boot
and every oxblood in my sight
to me did seem
the perfect setting for a foot
la crème de la crème de la crème
but now the style has hit the fashion floor
whichever way I turn
can't help but learn
the boots that I have seen I now can see no more

I used to look at those
along the Old Kent Road
heads shaven   boots laced tight
My mother bought my brother's pair
he told me it was like
walking on air
I was so proud he was the first
Black boy I know who loved them so
and so we had our fun until the bubble burst

We didn't know of uniforms or gangs
of racism or hate
fashion or fascist   National Front
we didn't know what it meant
In playgrounds we took up a bold defence
against the sticks and stones and names
always in a fight
Black and White
those were our games
along with British Bulldog   skipping
juggling and the like

Then Two-tone brought back Ska
intending to unite
roots reggae-loving Black
roots reggae-loving White

while in backstreet bars
some minds will fantasise
in bondage and in black
and think that boots have eyes

And what was once forbidden and taboo
uniform or fetish
is now part of British
mainstream fashion
I have seen them red and purple
emerald green in patent leather
I have seen them faded denim
I have even seen them glitter
but the worst I've seen are gingham

6-holes 8-holes 10-holes X-tongued X-rated
à la mode
stack-heeled square-toed
make a work boot look dated
A new design each week
to tempt the 90s chic
and yet
a standard pair
of black size 6 14-hole DMs
are hard to get
with toecaps made of steel and air cushion sole

Original designs are truly gems
beauty only moves me when it's rare
give me the simplest oldest boot and then
and only then I truly walk on air

The Black The White and The Blue

He's an East End Lad   East End Ed
East End born   East End bred
see his muscles   have a feel
Made in England   made of steel
East End lad   East End lad
square jaw   gift of the gab
packs a punch to find a clue
see his victims black   and blue

Black man   Asian man
flew from the East to East Ham
sun don't rise in East End cell
where Bangladesh meets English hell
hate mail   dog crap
midnight petrol bomb attack
sticks and stones and **PAKI GO HOME**
make his street a   no   go   zone

When Asian man dials 999
covered in blood of racist crime
police arrive   police arrest
the Asian man and kick his chest
and 666 the beast walks free
and **THE Sun** won't print what **THE Sun** won't see
BOYS IN BLUE BEAT BLACK MAN
cos Blue protects Blue whenever Blue can

PC White adds a stripe to his arm
the man suffers grievous bodily harm
they try to charge him for assault
'We had to restrain him it's all his fault'
PC Edward White   just an East End lad
with a chip on his shoulder of which he's proud
gotta be a hard nut come what may
so no-one will ever guess   that he's gay

26

East End lad   West End fag
same man   different drag
West End fag   West End fag
remembers the words of his East End dad
'This country's gone downhill over the years
and d'ya know why?' 'Why dad?' 'Niggers and queers.
Bring back hanging   that's what I say...
you could walk the streets without fear in my day...'

West End Eddie enters the club
looking attractive   looking for love
his eye lashes lowered his eye lingers long
on the man in the corner   muscular   bronze
At dawn when they leave it's erogenous zones
they have on their minds not the sticks and the stones
of the gang that attack   not the stainless steel
of their knives 'You queer bastards   how does this feel?'

East End lad   went up West
now oppressor   now oppressed
couldn't see in light of club
his big bronze man had Asian blood
East End blood on West End street
what will he say to his friends on the beat?
He can paint the town red but at dawn he'll pay
with a scar on his body that says 'I'm gay'

West End fag   West End fag
stabbed in the back by an East End lad
son of a racist left him for dead
boy in blue is covered in red
Black man   Asian man
kisses his lips and holds his hand
NIGGER   PAKI   QUEER
when will we walk the streets without fear?

Sentences

'I now pronounce you Man and Wife'
said the vicar 'You may kiss the bride'
and he raises her veil of gossamer white
and he kisses her lips
for he is a Man and she is a Wife
so for him to kiss her it is his right
and everyone smiles and the ring shines bright
on the finger where he placed it
and the family album reveals the white
teeth of the smile of the happily married couple
not her womanhood buried out of sight

So now their love is legitimate   legal
in the eyes of society   unequal

They begin to live their married life
they both go to work cos they have to survive
he spends his money on having fun outside
she spends hers on the home cos she is the wife
but the wedding presents make it alright
a microwave oven   a blender
and an excellent chopping knife

A syncopated heart beat
she's expecting a baby   their love is complete

And he comes home pissed from the pub one night
and she asks him why he's late
and he hates to be questioned about his life
he slaps her a bit to keep her quiet
she doesn't really put up a fight
then he puts it in her and pushes with all his might
and she closes her eyes and lips so tight
and when he's finished he turns off the light
covering up his huge   love   bite

And now their love is beginning to die
she loses the child and nobody questions why

And the years go by and she has to survive
though she often thinks of taking her life
she called the police round the other night
they took him in but they sympathised with him
then he says he's sorry and she thinks it's alright
and they say that his bark is worse than his bite
but she thinks of the bruises she has to hide
and she knows that that wedding camera lied
when it showed her smiling   fat   and   wide

And now their love has completely gone
but worse and worse the marriage goes on

And he comes home pissed from the pub one night
and she's gone to bed and turned off the light
and he turns it on again out of spite
and says 'Open your legs you bitch   it's my right
cos I'm a man and you're my wife'
so she punches him in the face with all her might
and leaves a bruise
but he holds her round the neck too tight
to be an embrace and he says
'If you do that again I'll fucking kill you   alright'

And now their love has changed to hate
and it seems like another age and time
that they went on that   first   shy   date

And her mother says 'He ought to be locked up inside'
and her father 'He should pick on someone his own size'
and her brother doesn't know what he's like
and her sister says 'Divorce him'
and she knows her sister's right
but she's scared what her man would do
and in spite of it all
she has her pride

And he comes home pissed from the pub one night
and he doesn't even speak
just beats her with his fists
and when she asks him why he has to fight
he says 'You're married to me for life'
then she knows that he knows that she spoke
to her solicitor on the phone the other night
And she cannot believe that this is her married life
he sees the hatred in her eyes
and he laughs and falls
and the last glimmer of hope inside her dies

She goes to the kitchen
and sees in the microwave oven
his dried up dinner
sees the broken blender
and the excellent chopping knife

The ring shines bright on the finger
where he placed it
but she holds the knife in her right
and when she stabs him
she stabs him with all her might
and anger

'I now pronounce you Man and Wife'
sentenced the vicar
the judge said 'Life'
and she turned in her grave
cos she knew she'd been sentenced
twice

Cain

I'm
not my brother's keeper
ball n chain
but baby
if you play abel
I'll be your cain
fratricide's my claim
to fame

count drac
precision bomber
of urban faeces
the inverted commas
around your suicide
helicop attack
genocidal maniac

I'm
white p o w d e r
white powder
whitepower
I met a morphose
in my ivory tower
whitehouse

I just killed
jimi janis JFK
lady day
OK
I'm
the white trigger fix
shot malcolm X
666
invisible letters
white lines
or urban decay K K

I'm
the H in the Haight vein
white high
back in 68
the smack crack
that attacks the black
widow stuck to the thread
of the web
of the welfare state
deadlock bed rock
sista streetwalker
caught in the wheel of fate
of a 69 9 9

I'm
pied piper
vampire viper
the thin white line
gonna make you mine

baby
they call me cain
don't take my name in vain

big brother
jealous lover
worship no other

E   (Manic Dance Mix A)

Turn on tune in
pop till you drop
you can't stop
pass go merry-go
happy-go human
relay race pace
bomb the bass
Ban the Bill
pop that pill
rave love-slave
pop your powdery
rose-hip pound
while time rolls
gold and round
60s theme 90s hit
6 and 9 in orbit
if you can't beat it
eat it   if you can't
mellow sell out
6+9 flip Pisces trip
Aquarius is hip
so spit out the pip

DJ G.O.D this is DJ G.O.D.
Creator of the Heaven and the E
Your manic MC M D M Λ
Director of   L   O   V   E

Hippyhippyhippyhippy
yippyippyippyippy
yuppy yuppi yuppie

Let there be lasers let there be
man made man made man
made man in my own image
free market enterprise LOVE
fruit of the factorytorytreetree

Miss First World

She's the advertisers dream   *Anorexia*
tall   white   slim   *bulimia*
eating a cream cake   *cream cake*
licking her lips hand on androgynous hips
the lady loves the lady loves to binge   *crisps*
She fancies chocolate milk and plain   *chocolate chip*
likes to unwrap her shame   *Coca Cola*
salivate and sate
feel full   *Princess Di's diet*
eat eject eradicate   *eat eject eradicate*
flesh flab fat   *flesh flab fat*

Forcing a finger down her throat   *First World Waste*
vesuvius   *Food mountains*
she   *huge hills of flesh*
tense
relaxes   *silicon tits*
peaks   *twin peaks*
Then flushed and spent   *small kleine petite*
splashes her marble face
she has high cheekbones   *throwing up*
and cherry lips   *vomiting*
                                      supermodel

She wears designer labels
mixes and mingles the perfect hostess   *Weight Watchers*
and mona lisa lifts her fork to eat   *XXL*
her dark expensive secret laced up tight *zero gravity*

ADVERTISING	Adolescents and adults binge on the artificial additives of capitalism
COMPULSIVE EATING	consumer goods crazes and clichés
DIETING	designer fads and E numbers economic growth and economic decline
MARKETING	talk of Third World famine but not the IMF eat plastic food get fat
OPERATING	get plastic surgery take amphetamines reduce se mettre au régime
VOMITING	binge vomit go on a diet
SLIMMING	to get thin slim svelte welcome Miss First World

Becoming A Nonymous

No more heroes anymore
no more heroes anymore

I was the first heroine
I put the K on pun
I used to dye my hair bright green
with purple spots and wear yellow
fishnet stockings with a seam
that met the crotch
I was obscene
I was a mid 70s scene
addict

Had my nose pierced twice
tattoo on my nipple
string knickers clung like a vice
wore my make-up neat
eye liner bin-liner
didn't know who I was
but I knew
I was some one

When I looked in the mirror
it smashed I looked so bad
it was good
You want history
read my horror story

I was a cidic
an archic
archaic prosaic
anti es tab lish ment arian ism
they couldn't throw me in prison

Piss in my glass or spunk
I was a mid 70s queen
of punk

Then one day I decided to get a job in a bank
I scraped my hair back into a bow
I tried to say 'No'
but found myself walking the plank
It was 83 when my roots went black
I saw a peculiar face looking back
in the mirror
I thought 'Shit   that's it'

Then they put my salary up
i was becoming a yuppie
and i had to wear a dark blue skirt
below the knee
i was becoming a
nightmare   and i couldn't recognise
my friends any more and they couldn't recognise
me   i was becoming a
nonymous

Then i bought a flat and did it up
and gave yet another dinner party
it's the same old horror story
and kept looking in the mirror
and getting older
and my i   dentity
was flaking and cracking up

Then i got a man a marriage a mortgage
no.2 2.2 kids   i was too wrapped up
in bringing them up to see my face
fade   like a pressed flower de
pressed be   tween two volumes that never met

Then i opened my cupboard door
and saw my past fall out in chains
and they took it away and locked it up

And how can i say i haven't got enough
when nothing is left of the horror any more?

London's Burning

The anti-poll tax people say
CAN'T PAY   WON'T PAY
left   right   left   right
march   march
we're hitting the road   we're hitting the bins
cos tomorrow the hated tax begins
the Left the Right the Black the White
march   march

From Lambeth five hundred and forty-eight
to Westminster with it's royal estate
Maggie   Maggie   Maggie
OUT   OUT   OUT
Maggie   Maggie   Maggie
OUT   OUT   OUT
Maggie OUT Maggie OUT
Maggie   Maggie   Maggie
OUT   OUT

Outside no.10 Downing Street
the crowd sit down in protest
against this mockery
of democracy that by law
helps the rich to rob the poor
yes   this poll tax transcends politics
the Left the Right oppose its threat
but it's illegal to sit in the street
in peaceful protest   YOU'RE UNDER ARREST
sticks and bottles are flying
the horses are charging
and London's burning   London's burning

Community charge community attack
community charge community attack
banners are banned   riot shields
are wielded as weapons
as we fall down get up   fall down get up

cos we're anti-poll tax
and our chant is still intact

Maggie   Maggie   Maggie
OUT   OUT

Outside the South African Embassy
someone sets fire to the adjacent building
London's burning   London's burning
and we are told to move back by eyes of hatred
and we hate back
and we are pushed back
hard as Hillsborough
until we become one person united
and still they are crushing the poor
and we are paying their wages
and today they are paying for it
their morality is our mortality

NO POLL TAX   NO POLL TAX

A police van accelerates into the crowd
on the south side
Outside the National Gallery
I am raised to the sky   my bag falls   crash
BROKEN GLASS
WE'LL GET YOU FOR THAT
Will someone paint this scene
and display it for posterity?

They are getting carried away
I am carried away   split
into six clenched fists
one on each arm   the third has my feet
YOU FUCKING BITCH she says
and they offer me struggling
to the god of law
but I fall free   again they grab
somehow evidence is on my side

I find the words to state my defence
my case is dropped onto the paving slab

Maggie   Maggie   Maggie
OUT   OUT

Outside in St Martins Lane
someone sets fire to a Jaguar
flames rage into complacent sky
London's burning   London's burning

Outside Tower Records in Regent Street
someone breaks the law
it makes a beautiful pattern
it happens again and again and
every shop window is a spider's web

London's burning   London's burning

Outside in Westminster
OUT   OUT
Outside in Westminster
OUT   OUT
Outside in Westminster

London's burning
London's burning
London's burning
London's burning

It's My Party

I was born in 79
when I came out I was covered in slime
mummy suffered no labour this time
'Mother and baby doing fine'
didn't learn to speak but I learnt how to whine
my first word was 'Money'
and then I learnt the party line
never learnt to walk but I learnt how to climb

I was born with no silver spoon in my mouth
but that's the way I speak
I stole lunches from the other kids
I had more than enough to eat
Teacher made me milk monitor
I gave myself a rise
sold each bottle for 20p
and called it 'Enterprise'

I was born in 79
never learnt to walk but I learnt how to climb
I owned a house by the time I was nine
you see that car over there   it's mine
I got stocks and shares and I'll sign on the dotted
line if it makes me money
I don't have any friends cos I don't have time
I'll stab you in the back if you'll scratch mine

I was born quite comfortable
but now I live in luxury
occasionally I'll open house
so people can suck up to me
I live in an all-white suburb
oh it's not that I'm a racist
I respect good breeding and serious wealth
in all sorts of far away places

I was born in 79
I'll stamp on your culture if you'll embrace mine
I'll give you a job if you'll stand in line
and you'll get no extra for overtime
Why are you going on strike   you swine
d'you expect me to pay you more money?
Your working conditions are just fine
and your salary   dear   will never reach mine

I was born into a family
that managed to make ends meet
and I really believe that if you're poor
you should stand on your own two feet
We paid our dustman extra
to take away our waste
so when I see you rifling through bins
it fills me with distaste

I was born in 79
I go to the city   I call it my shrine
for the inner cities I don't have time
they smell too much and don't sell the right wine
I like Opera   but the Arts are in decline
they don't make enough money
just jumped up socialists ranting in rhyme
or attacking the State cos they're that way inclined

I was born into a family
that's the way that God intended
marriage   and any other 'family'
set-up is pretended
If you don't accept our social laws
then we'll introduce more clauses
to prevent you from converting kids
or promoting your sick causes

I was born in 79
I was born to rule with a Right Divine
I'm here to wage a war on crime
I'll pay police more to make you do time
even if they resort to lying
we've allocated money
but as to the unemployed or the dying
they can whistle and they can whine

I was born a healthy baby
and I've managed to combat illness
so if you're sick you should eat better food
not that supermarket rubbish
smoke less   drink less
but keep the revenue high
and if you're home less
I suggest you shut up and die

I was born in 79
in 1990 I had to resign
but don't be fooled   though the face isn't mine
we haven't swerved from the party line
you're welcome to watch on tv us wine
and dine at my party   your money
cos it's my party   mine   mine   mine
I'm thirteen today and I'm doing just fine

Blonde Bombshell Defused

She did it for the money she did it for the glory
from MP to PM she put the Tory back in History

She sold her story to **THE Sun**
BLONDE BOMBSHELL DEFUSED
Attractive blonde 65
tells of home affairs that led to Party divide

'John was like a son to me
until we did it on the back seat of his car
and suddenly he became more than the boy next door
John was cool   I was sultry
but he ran the bath while I ran the country
He was witty but elusive'
she tells **THE Sun EXCLUSIVE**

'He lived at no.11   I was at no.10
but even then it wasn't easy
Cecil found out and was furious
and Norman was jealous
I began to take a belt into meetings
and had to resort to the odd beating
I would even lock away their favourite blow-up toys
Boys will be boys   they say

Our passion was eating the cake and having it
and we often made love in the cabinet
devising new and devious ways of screwing the poor
John preferred to leave the door open
hoping someone would come before he did
I wanted more than that

I knew about the plot I knew about the danger
"I fight to win" I cried "I fight to win John Major"

I sent for my own Whips to whip me
with my honourable permission they began to unzip me

those men in grey suits they wanted to try on my dress
cos they knew I put the S&M into M&S
then John rang to say "Have you nominated me yet?"
I said "Yes"

So like three blind mice they ran
so that I could secure the partnership with my man.
I signed on   the humiliation John took my old position
and formally moved next door to no.10 Downing Street
I allowed a few photogenic tears to roll down my cheek

It's a hard life living off the pension of the State
and the Queen   the bitch   refuses to abdicate
so now we take the back seat just like that first time
that John's grey hairs mingled and mixed with mine

Some may say John's a nonentity   well he's meant to be
if no-one can recognise his face or remember his name
then we won't get the blame   will we?

As for another woman in the cabinet
I really had to draw the line
Well he's mine he's my own man
I sacrificed a great deal to put him in my place
I even left the Nottingham lace table cloths
that's the extent of my love

John has excellent street cred
and he's all for a classless society
where individuals climb that vertical hierarchy
and we discuss controversial issues in bed
like "What does one say when they shout
Johnny   Johnny   Johnny
OUT   OUT   OUT?"...'

And so now on the surface at least
the Tories are united in matro-monetary bliss
Thatcher puts the whip back in her handbag
And Major puts the Tory back in His

Money Talks

Wake   wash   dress   bus
tube   work   home   bed
wake   wash   dress   bus
tube   work   home   bed

Rolling in money?
I'm rolling over in bed
I don't want to get ahead in
marketing or advertising
all those people spend their lives in
queues   to climb the ladder to abuse
You're giving me an offer I can't refuse
but a company won't comfort me
when all I see are spots before my eyes
on ties   the noose around the neck
for the sake of a pay cheque
money talks but it lies

Money talks
you hear it on the Stock Exchange
when the Pound goes crash
and there's no remains
and the company's complaining
that they haven't made a profit
so they dock your pay or sack you
then they talk to you
Come off it

Money talks
you hear it on The Underground
in the middle of the tunnel
when the tube breaks down
it is so much inhibited
it really is pathetic
an entire generation
under general anaesthetic

Chorus

Rolling in money?
I'm rolling over in bed
I'm not MD I'll wear DMs instead
If you're talking zones
then One must be the worst for clones
see them coming out of the tube
cut the air with a knife
it's so thick with fumes
Perhaps the air makes them brain dead
W1 they double your fare
but you can't beg money
cos money talks and it closes it's eyes
Yes money talks but it lies

Money talks dress bus tube
work home bed
money talks dress bus tube
work home bed
It tells you all the things that
money can buy
but it's an optical illusion
now you see it now you die

R.A.W.

UNCOOKED
UNCUT
UNCAGED
UNCHAINED
UNCENSORED

Uncooked uncut uncaged unchained uncensored

R.A.W.
rhythm and word
uncooked uncut
uncaged unchained
uncensored

Raw
sucking out the marrow
of a word
from a bone
holding up a mirror
cos RAW is
WAR
fighting for your rights
in an unjust world

I'm not putting on a wig
for this court case
no make-up on my face
I don't want to attract
only to attack
not to cause a fight
but fight a cause
no time to pause
I'm a poet
it's a four-letter word

I could write about the trees
and the flowers
but I write about roots
rap is my delivery   raw
more bitter than sweet
more twisted than bitter
no throw away words
cos I never drop litter

Poetry is theft
a fact
I'm a word kleptomaniac
I know about the theft act
accuse me of that
if rimes a crime
rap is crap
I don't believe in that
Black people had a history
stolen from them
and we're claiming it
back

cos
they took our languages away
made us pray
to a god with no pigment
a figment of a sick imagination
story of creation flipped
tricked
and no reparation
Ignored the colour of their lord
but when we sang the gospel
it was raw
Rich though they started out poor
at death's white door
Bessie 'n' Billie
they knew the score

Chorus

When we screamed the Black blues
'n' soul   when we belted out
belowthebeltjellyrocknrolljazzfunk
wasn't just about sex 'n' junk
if you want a white parallel
look at the politics of punk
When we entertain   we edutain
articulate the pain
of our ancestors' ball 'n' chain
rubbing raw on our psyche
Black culture goes deeper
than X and Nike

Chorus

and raw is rap
taking our languages back
using our own black words
and being heard
it's a political act
to dis the system
with less tune to distract
Those who say
too much slang
we can't understand
calling for rap to be banned
ignore the fact
that R.A.W. is RAP
and RAP is RAW
and RAW means WAR

Chorus

Rap Trap

Black
young and gifted
your politics shifted
used to be a giver
now you're floating down the river
like driftwood
sold your soul for a deal
the big black badman
sexist appeal
get real
not so long ago they used to lynch ya
now that you've sung well-hung
get the picture?
Rap to rape
might be your fantasy escape
but look what they did to the ape
in the RAP-TRAP

Slack
went the rhymes
when you signed on the dotted line
dot   dot   dot
now you can't find rewind
heard it on the grapevine
rape-line BT urinal
you pimp your sisters on vinyl
Black man rapper
Black man ragga ragga Shabba
did you lay down that track
or was it Abba?
Money Money Money
you're a slave to the lyrical trade
'cept now you're getting paid
in the RAP-TRAP

Snap
went the trap
when you starred in the video show
3D went your stereo ego
rich man gangsta man
shooting up the hood
you're wading through the river
of your mother and your sister's
menstrual blood
and there's no looking back
and you're selling your brothers your slack
rhymes with free-base
Uncle Tom with a hard-on
disgracing the race
in the RAP-TRAP

Stings Like a Bee

Hieroglyphic lyrics
rekindle the embers
of free Black spirits

Hip   hop   hip
hyp   hop
hypnotic rap rhythm
rocks from the lips
of the slave ships
The Griot grits images
of skeleton villages
and the Monkey sits Stackolee
in the African American tree-top
trying to outwit
the king of the concrete jungle

Black man badman gambler pimp
he twists his gun-tongue
around a rhyme of disrespect
for the next man or woman
Plays the Dozens for a dime
or a dope-smoke in the Oral
Tradition of griotic hypnotic
rap rhythm

Signifying Monkey   Stackolee
MC Muhammad Ali
floats like a butterfly
stings like a   be-bop beat-box
Run-D.M.C.   Chuck D
U.N.I.T.Y. Queen Latifah
be-bop hip hop

Hypnotic rap rhythm
heart rocks the cradle
of history herstory

RAPunzel

Not once but
twice upon a time coz you ain't heard my speak
this ain't no fairy tale   this is reality
live in a tower block   call it hell
but it never get me down my name is RAPunzel
The lift never works an it smells of piss
I'm tellin ya sis   it can't go on like this
My auntie says 'I'm getting old   I can't make the stair
RAPunzel   RAPunzel   let down ya hair'

I tried the weavin   tried the waxin
hot comb   curly perm and relaxin
hair meant to grow but nothin hapnin
filled with a dread that I am a baldhead
So she trudge an she trudge an she trudge to meet me
she hum a tune and she read graffiti
she's busy   she's getting dizzy
I'm so ashamed that my hair is short and frizzy

An a man stands   on the ground floor
don't know what he's hangin aroun for
he serenades me   with Public Enemy
he's crazy   or is he?
He seems to like me   I say politely
'Come up and see me   if you dare'
'*RAPunzel   RAPunzel   let down ya hair*'

Then I have an idea
I take a trip ta Dalston   then ta Brixton
never have no money for no hair decoration
stay in the undergroun and rap like hell
I gotta use my head my name is RAPunzel
I need a twenty metre hair extension
thought I'd mention   ain't no pretension
wholesale   retail   strong enough to abseil
gals get plaitin   RAPunzel's rappin

Home   an sittin in my easy chair
'RAPunzel   RAPunzel   LET DOWN YA HAIR'

Now he climb an he climb an he climb to meet me
he got a brand new rap to treat me
Urggh he's ugly   but he loves me
looks ain't everything can't see him when he hugs me
I try to tease him   I try to relax him
slot his favourite track in   nothin hapnin
all brawn no brain   think I'll axe him
he's borin   I'm snorin   nex mornin

'Auntie   keep hummin that tune
Mr Public Enemy's comin soon
Get out the scissors now   he's there'
'RAPunzel   RAPunzel   LET DOWN YA HAIR'
We gather the hair in a great big bundle
liberate RAPunzel   I ain't no damsel
chuck this vanity   throw it out the window
keep my sanity   no good for him though

He's OK   just a bit shaken
think he's got the message if I ain't mistaken
not my type   even though I like
Don't Believe the Hype

I say 'Auntie   ya gotta good sensa rhythm
we're gonna win em   us women
get out the ghetto   ain't no lookin
back   you backin   me rappin'
She say 'Daughter   thought ya'd never ask
we gonna live it happy ever after
pack ya bag   clear ya head   check this soun
Ya let down ya hair now ya gonna let ya hair down'

Twice upon a time check   this women
this ain't the endin   it's the beginnin
Twice upon a time check   this men
does ya hair stand   on end?

55

Sex Is

Some like it with a he
some like it with a she
some like to use the four-letter words
and LOVE is a many splendoured thing
but some like to stick to three and
some like it O.T.T.
some like to kiss
sex is   sex is

Straight sex is recreation
same sex a revelation
SM sex negotiation
safe sex is masturbation
some like it in
some like it out
some like in out in out
. and think that that's what it's all about

Sex is a thing you think of
when you're feeling warm and free
often it goes hand in hand
with sexuality
sex is what you think it is
there's no authority
helps you to lose and find yourself
that's how it's meant to be

Chorus

Sex is the talk of the nation
sex is under legislation
sex is what society's based on
sex is misinformation
sex is an excuse to be a sexist
sex is an excuse to be a rapist
anti-gay and lesbians   racist
sex is   sex is

Women are said to ask for it
if their skirts are above the knee
Africa and gay men are blamed
for causing HIV
few at the top control our thoughts
throughout our history
and those whom they fear from ignorance
they call minority

Some like it with a he
some like it with a she
some like to think we should all conform
to the nuclear family
some like to charge a fee
but some pocket the money
and make a business
sex is   sex is

Some like to get a hard-on
some wear designer condoms
some call it contraception
some STD protection
some don't have anything to put it on
some cope with menstruation
it's all of this
sex is   sex is

Chorus

Some think it's A.C.E.
some stay A.L.O.N.E.
some want L.O.V.E.
sex is   sex is
basis of society
sex is   sex is
something we must set free
sex is   sex is

It's Better Post- than Pre-

I'm sitting on this toilet seat
I'm reading graffiti
and some of it's political
and some of it is cheeky
but I only see red
coz I'm feeling rather freaky
when it comes to having PMT
no woman can beat me
I'm speedy   I'm angry
I'm horny   I'm stoned
I want to be touched
and I WANNA BE LEFT ALONE
PMT I pick my target
PMT I start to load
PMT I pull my trigger
my tits are ready to explode

Stick em on   stick em in   stick em up gals
stick em on   stick em in   stick em up
if you wanna shoot an arrow
then it's time to load your barrel
stick em on   stick em in   stick em up

I remember that first memory
a dark red stain
I didn't feel no nausea
I didn't feel no pain
I was a woman   a warrior
erotic   arcane
and once a month a lunatic
in nappies and insane
My mum she bought the towels in
she didn't make a fuss
she told me about men
and she said 'It's them and us'
mini   regular
Super   SUPER PLUS

58

I stuck em on   I stuck em in
and then I stuck em up

Stick em on   stick em in   stick em up gals
stick em on   stick em in   stick em up
if you wanna sate your lust
then insert a Super Plus
stick em on   stick em in   stick em up

Remember waiting in the queue
to pay for that first pack
you're looking at the ceiling
with your hands behind your back
then it's you and the assistant
who's since got the sack
says 'DOCTOR WHITE'S MINI PRESS-ON TOWELS
how much are they Jack?'
Or you're sitting on the toilet seat
one hand between your thighs
the other with instructions
on how to DIY
you hop skip and jump about
you ought to win a prize
and your entire extended family
are queuing up outside

Stick em on   stick em in   stick em up gals
stick em on   stick em in   stick em up
if you're paranoid in public
I can't find a better subject
stick em on   stick em in   stick em up

They have adverts on the telly
to say they are discreet
disposable   collapsible
invisible   and neat
the ones that make you sit as if
you're one of the elite

and ones that give you ATTITUDE
when walking down the street
The ones that won't go down the loo
however much you try
that bloated towel or tampon
that simply will not die
and some that leak and some you like
and they're the ones you buy
if you're cool rosé is quite passé
you stick to extra-dry

Stick em on   stick em in   stick em up gals
stick em on   stick em in   stick em up
if you're thinking of your image
then forget about your spillage
stick em on   stick em in   stick em up

Well some call it PMS
and some call it PMT
some say it's a deficiency
of vitamin B
some say it is a myth
some say it is reality
but those of us who have it know
it's better post-   than pre-
some call it The Curse
from the story of Creation
the Time of the Month
or just menstruation
for the past   the present
and the future generation
I think it's time we gave ourselves
a STANDING OVULATION

Stick em on   stick em in   stick em up gals
stick em on   stick em in   stick em up
if you're paranoid in public
I can't find a better subject
stick em on   stick em in   stick em up

Rappin It Up

I was in a bar once
eyeing up the cocktails
waiting for a friend of mine
won't bore you with the details
when I hear a voice
that is gettin me annoyed
it sounds like 'Mind if I join you?'
Peace destroyed
'This seat taken?
What's your name?' 'Patience'
'Saw you coming out
of the Underground station
Get you a drink?' 'No'
'Do you come here oft' 'Yes'
'What d'you do?'
I said 'I am a poetess'   He said

'Funny you should say that
Fancy a quick one?
Write a bit myself ya know
get yer lips round this one
I wandered lonely as a cloud'
So I drank down my drink
and I said it out aloud
'I walked on my own
from the Underground station
listenin to the beauty
of my own imagination
happy jus being
alone in my head
so don't give me a line
from a poet that's dead'

Coz I'm rappin it up in a real tight squeeze
I don't cross my i's   I don't dot my t's
Wordsworth   Milton   line them up
an they're dead   I am PA an I am rappin it up

I was at a gig once
listen to the ska-beat
jivin an writhin
an hot with a body heat
when I feel an arm
that is gettin me annoyed
and the hot sweaty fingers
I learn to avoid
'Mind if I join you?
Really find you sexy
Saw you dancin on yer own
and thought I'd introduce me
Get you a drink?' 'No'
'Have we met before?' 'Yes'
'What d'ya do?'
I said 'I am a poetess'   He said

'Funny you should say that
we ought to get it going
I've spent my whole life
jus writing one poem
a masterpiece
it's called *Paradise Lost*'
and the beat slowed down
and the music stopped
I said 'I skanked on my own
to the ska-beat music
lovin every minute
till ya came to abuse it
grabbin an clawing
an pushin an pawing
I don't give a shit
about your master poem'

Coz I'm rappin it up in a real tight squeeze
I don't cross my i's   I don't dot my t's
Milton   Shakespeare   line them up
an they're dead   I am PA an I am rappin it up

62

I was at the disco
listen to the hip hop
head was a buzzing
so I thought it never would stop
Along comes Shakespeare
and the Boys
an it's 'Lock up yer daughters
I'm the King of Noise'
He stands on the stage
and begins a recitation
A to Z
of a famous quotation
not a spark
originality
they ain't clappin they're nappin
so listen to me

I said 'Get off the stage
and go home to your bed
coz I am alive
and you are dead
An when you try to speak
your words are obsolete
while I communicate right from ya
head down to ya feet'

Because I'm rappin it up in a real tight squeeze
I don't cross my i's   I don't dot my t's
Shakespeare   Milton   Pope and Dryden
Wordsworth   Eliot   Great Tradition
all you poets I don't give a fuck
coz you're dead   I am PA an I am RAPPIN IT UP

Other poetry available from Gecko Press

JADE REIDY: **Lust**

A collection of explicitly poetical, perversely pro-
found and intricately personal poems, dancing with a
vital sexual force that commands, illuminates and sin-
uously weaves its way through the contradictions of
sexual identity and personal history, towards a place
of quiet inner power.

64 pages: £5.95 ISBN 0 9524067 0 5

JOHN ANSTISS: **Butch Boy**

A celebration of gay life being richly lived. John
Anstiss takes us from the early relationship with his
father into urban territory where sex, death and
homophobic violence are written about with a wit
and clarity that demand attention. His commanding
stage presence and resonant voice fairly leap off these
pages, assaulting the mind and senses.

64 pages: £5.95 ISBN 0 9524067 5 6